LIB

September 2

T0060484

2

If we have
no peace,
it is because we
have forgotten
that we belong
to each other.

✧ Mother Teresa ✧

ROSE

Libra

I will speak my mind

Ω

autumn

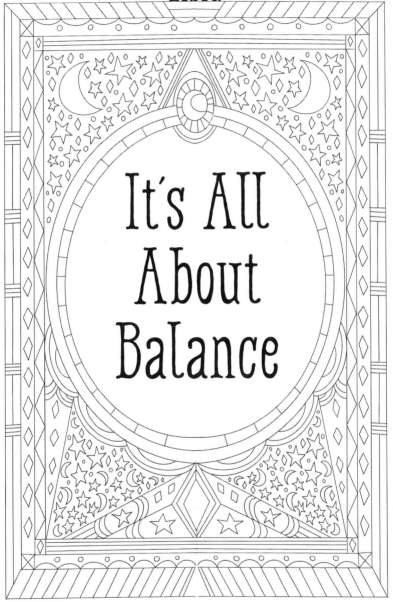

It's All
About
Balance

Libra

Ruled by Venus

Creative

CHARMING

STYLISH

DIPLOMATIC

Witty

RULING HOUSE

7

The House of Partnerships

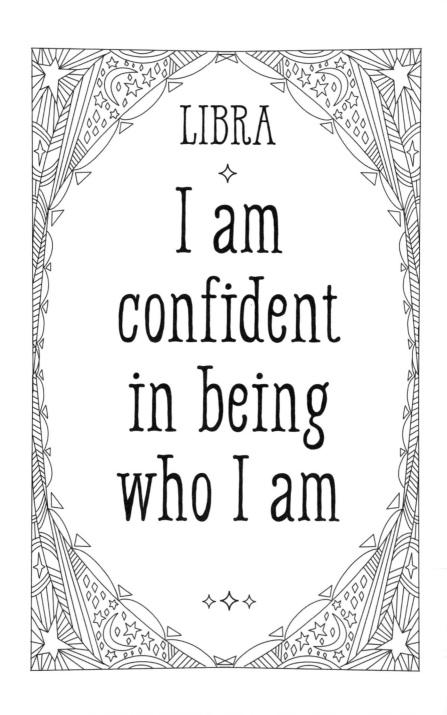

LIBRA

I am
confident
in being
who I am

LIBRA

Aries

Taurus

Gemini

Cancer

Leo

Virgo

Libra

Scorpio

Sagittarius

Capricorn

Aquarius

Pisces

Air Signs

Aquarius

Libra

Gemini